the RELIEF of AMERICA

DIANE GLANCY

TIA CHUCHA PRESS, CHICAGO

Acknowledgment to *Agni Review* for "Buffalo Jump, Blue Mounds, Minnesota"; *The Wisconsin Review* for "Hearing about the Mystery Lights while on a Bus near Joplin, Missouri"; *Coe Review* for "We Stop by a Farm near Wytheville, Virginia"; *Paper Radio: a journal of experimental arts* for "Stopping at a McDonald's in Alabama"; *Permafrost* for "Cinnamon Bear"; *Mankato Review* for "Black Hawk"; *Blue Pitcher* for "Relief"; The Colorado Review for "Palace of the Plains"; *Oxalis* for "After-image"; *Lynx* for "Democracy on Wheels"; *North Stone Review* for "A Walk on a Country Road"; *New Letters* for "Christopher"; *Reed Magazine* for "Oklahoma Land Run"; *Palo Alto Review* for "History of the Homeland"; *Potpourri, a Magazine of the Literary Arts* for "Flight 532 - Houston to Mpls" and "Treatment" (under the title "500 Years"); *Dominion Review* for "How in Spite of Us It Works"; *Husk* for "How in Spite of Us It Works"; *Pacific Coast Journal* for "Pledge of America" and "Giving the Air Away"; *Potomac Review* for "A Script called Birth"; *Pemmican* for "*Two Forms*, Henry Moore, Philadelphia Museum of Art"; *Amelia* for "Stone Figure from an Ancient Dynasty"; *Wolf Head Quarterly* for "Sweezo" and "Independence Hall"; *Red Weather* for "Cartography"; *Footwork: the Paterson Literary Review* for "The Day before Christmas." "Christopher" also appears in the *XVIII Pushcart Prize Anthology,* Bill Henderson, editor. "America" appears in *After the Storm, Poems on the Persian Gulf War,* edited by Jay Meek and F. D. Reeve, Maisonneuve Press, Washington, D.C. "The Relief of America" was read on the television broadcast, *Book TV C-Span2, The Poetry Society of America's, What's American about American Poetry?* I thank the National Federation of State Poetry Societies for their awards to "The Hands" and "American Leaf." The poems appear in the annual anthologies. I thank the Arts and Humanities Council of Tulsa for a grant which made part of this manuscript possible. I also thank the National Endowment for the Arts.

Printed in the United States of America.

Library of Congress Catalog Card Number: 00-130212.

BOOK DESIGN: Jane Brunette
COVER ART: From *Pre-Hispanic Mexican Stamp Designs,*
   by Frederick V. Field, Dover Publications
BACK COVER PHOTO: Larry Gus

Published by:
Tia Chucha Press
A Project of the Guild Complex
PO Box 476969
Chicago IL 60647

Distributed by:
Northwestern University Press
Chicago Distribution Center
11030 South Langley Avenue
Chicago IL 60628

Tia Chucha Press and the Guild Complex have received support from the John D. and Catherine T. MacArthur Foundation, Lannan Foundation, Sara Lee Foundation, National Endowment for the Arts, the Illinois Arts Council, Kraft Foods, City of Chicago Department of Cultural Affairs, Lila Wallace-Readers Digest Fund, Eric Mathieu King Fund of the Academy of American Poets, The Chicago Community Foundation, the Reva and David Logan Foundation, the Illinois Humanities Council, Poets & Writers, The Woods Fund of Chicago, WPWR-TV Channel 50 Foundation, The Mayer and Morris Kaplan Family Foundation, Driehaus Foundation, the Elizabeth F. Cheney Foundation and individual donors.

CONTENTS

▼I▼

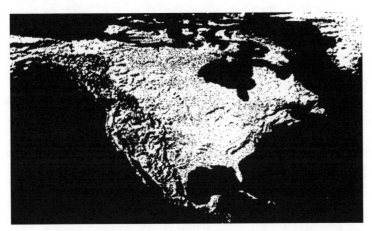

North America is an Indian's head. Growling. The Great Lakes for an eye. Florida and the Gulf for nose and open mouth. Roach of the western mountain range.

Well. It was difficult when the buffalo left. We heard them singing from the next world. The sun sat like a turnip on the edge of the table. They sang their hearts out and we were blessed.

Oh little buffalo lost in our laps. Sing O kee oooo O hok ee and one half-faced growl will last.

"Mapping America remains a slippery business."

"MAPPING AMERICA FROM ODD ANGLES," SANFORD PINSKER

▼I▼

For David

and

for America

(I think she's looking more like Mammy Yokum)

▼I▼

Christopher

Here come Christopher Columbus comming ober t' wabes.
PUFF. PUFF.
He think he come to the segund part of urth.
His shups bump inter land at night
y haze la senal dla cruz.
Hey Yndias. He say. *HEY ERMERICA.*
He brang glaz beads & bells.
Luego se ayunto alli mucha gente dla Isla.
We think he god from skie. Yup. Yup. Wedu.
The blue oshen sprad like a table napkin by his shups.
Como el por ante todos toma
va como de hecho tomo possession dla dha.
Yaz. He say. I take. *Now whar find GOLD?*
Our har like harsehair. He say.
He look our fish tooth on spears. *HAR HAR.* He laf.
Los reyes wand gold. *Gloria religion xpiana.*
Gloria Yndias. He say. Y load his shups. Wedu.
Thar go Christopher. Huf. Huf.
Wid gold he own t' segund urth.
Wid gold he buy our souls inter heaben.

Treatment

They show up
eyes red with saltwater and scurvy
December new world snows to the lip

Land their church house \ larder \ scabbards
petunia plates and monkey whips

They freezing \ borrow animal skins \ corn
squash \ we give them land \ parcels
of hope

Ears froze nose doze well they dig
the new world can't go back
English gentlemens \ indentured Toe Joes
now farmer \ baker \ Indian maker \ they digging graves
faster than anything

Scabrous
the denting machines \ teapots
the milking on 3 legged stools

We hear their new world hop \ Jesus \ salve woir
Get you BACK we say \
Amsterdamning

Now wagons westward hoe
the horse dances \ fields of wheat in Kansas

They eat rodeo hotdogs \ grape freezes
haven't they bought enough totems from one
trading post or another \ ashtrays
the shape of states \ cedar boxes \ walnuts
Indians wrapped in blankets
clouds we can see through \ O
haven't they had enough

Pig lassos \ hurdy gurdys \ trucker stops \ now the
white-faced steers watch from the pasture
cow horns on the quarter moon
sorghum and the likes \ crannies of Evinrudes

A Johnson City Texas Saturday night \ cape the apers
wrestling buzzing wuggles
rock and holy rollers

All horns in New York \
where pigeons with red feet cross Central Park
\ the painting at the Met
Christ after Flogging \ the red marks on his back
the same as pigeons' feet

O work ethic and label-savers
lighthouse to nasturtiums
America \ fields ajar.

Cartography

If I put a pencil in your paw
and helped you hold it
you could draw what you're thinking.
We'd move the pencil.
No more than you're comfortable with.
You could make a circle
and I would think of the head
of a mouse or bird you bit off and left
on the walk.
You could draw a line and I would guess
what you meant.
How it feels never to laugh.
Maybe you could hold the pencil in your mouth
to tell me of the peripheral fields
in the scythe of your yellow eyes,
the hayfork of your teeth.
Precious lamb, take the pencil,
mark your colonial fields,
your revolutionary storage bins and pantry.
Your whole map.

Buffalo Jump, Blue Mounds, Minnesota

A rusted gate opens the place.
The gentle grass waving like a man with hand-signals
guiding a plane to its gate.
The itch of birdnoise all over.
The swarm of wind like a nest of bees.
The cliff where Indians stampeded buffalo to their kill.
The Indians themselves would feel it,
Dakotas, I suppose here, or Chippewa.
Their swift fall into mission schools.
The buffalo traveling ahead of their bodies now.
The slight adjustment to altitude something like panic.
Maybe roller skates slipping on their feet,
the rink floor several hundred feet down,
and they going. The wide sky over,
the great husk opened like walnuts from their shells.
I pick up a rock thinking it's a polished tool,
a hide-scraper no doubt, a worked-stone
slick with the feel of first-ground not under foot.
But walk on faith now, the missionary said,
just spread your arms and walk.

Independence Hall

Restored \ they tell us. The gray walls just like they found them under 40 coats or so of paint \ it seemed so anyway \ scraping to the primal coat. A storm-bank low on the sky. How else do we get to the unexpected? The something we wish wasn't there. Our country defined by words \ just what they meant \ and how was written before conditions that would carry the country with significance. Take calipers now and measure frankly the years since the papers moved along the last edge of the table. The wars \ the add-ons \ the ramps of America \ trailer of nations \ the whole lot. Again the alley behind the house when snow gets old with cars \ a dead solid gray \ before electricity \ the force hitting the earth \ an asteroid \ the near miss of it \ we've been bumped before \ lost dinosaurs that way \ not the old wreck parked in the backyard \ but the construent \ gray walls packed with an extension cord \ the amendments \ something close to them after all.

Cedars wander from cemeteries on a sandy strip
of prairie. Cows graze in the shinnery.
After supper the truck walks through the field.
Every *mooo* a despair and children with not even
milk money. The hard knocks. Set backs.
Only too entirely school-like.
The knuckles rapped by a jumping door-handle
or a knob for rolling up windows.
In the flat distance the wind spits trucks
like peas into shooters.
The bull roams the field.
His wild eye butting the barbed wire
until the farmer rounds him up, markets him.
The swathing, baling, the trips to the granary.
The café at dawn where farmers open the light
with their talk.
The land still at the same work.
Rubbing them out, swallowing boxes of them
just barely underground
while their grain reaches higher in the air.

Stone Figure from an Ancient Dynasty
FREER GALLERY, SMITHSONIAN

Even in stone your stomach protrudes.
Your teeth clench. Your face grimaces.
Hands braced on thighs. You still bear
a corner of the temple though its weight is gone.
You squat like an umpire behind home-plate.
Your strange mouth ready to call, *OUT* or *SAFE.*

You got our squaw corn.
Stripped flint corn.
Red flour corn. Soft white corn.
Our blue corn.
Nuetta sweet corn. Pod corn.
Short ear dent corn.
The purple sunflower and pumpkin.
They're growing all over your yards and house.
The white lima bean.
Yellow bean. Pinto.
Calico bean.
Brown tepary bean.
Hominy and tobacco.
Yes. You got it all now in your furrows. You even know when light says it will be another hour. You're the Hourists who thought of time. You got it, Chickie. The whole wax. The Pow Wowists can't sit back like you. *Whee Choo.* All tickies twanging for you. The Great Hour of Hope is yours, baby. The Hipped. We're the humble bee, Bubba. The Whipped. The stars and stripes stripped. The old Geronimo death cry. No licorice stick for our sweet teeth. It's a black rope lasso for us, cowpoke. Under your ingenious grip. You even shut off dark. Bring lightbulbs to the night. Eyeballs of the spirits. *Zote. Whazzotta!* Yours be do. Our burden basket. Corniefields. Kachina carnie clowns. Indivisible. American Bull says *Liberty be yous.*

In the second story of the farmhouse
up under the storm
the thunder milks lightning from the sky
trees consistently jump with wind.
I think how the country is too much for one
person the upheaval of the first story
the rural stemwork shooting corn
and squash from the ground.
Down the county road in town
its antique store-front windows rattle
cut-out farmhouses
on cardboard fields.
In the square of disobedience
the old voices pound their wisdom.
They escape from a corner of the universe
to say to the storm we carve our high points
the wires of clothesline
the woodcross of every farmyard.

We Stop by a Farm near Wytheville, Virginia

The man on a tractor plows the field.
His corn waits under the narrow sill
of his eye.
Cars pass his field
and rise like arms through
mountain tunnels. The noise of the tractor
taps the breathless air.
His eyes hold the stalks upright like small
children.

Relief

When his throat clogged
like a gas can with a cloth in its mouth,
he called out to the Rocky Mountains
and Appalachian.
I put a prayer rag on his car,
started it on empty
and took him to the doctor with a right.

I gave him my hand with fingers calm as farmponds
reflecting the moon.
We needn't faunch.
Doesn't coyote carry us on his saddlebag?

If there was rain he simply put up the tarp
and slept under it,
dropped the American flag like pants for a shot.

A sore throat can bring a man to his elbows.

The sticky medicine dried like spit-up
on a chenille robe.
One of those ribbed mothers
that feels like armadillo.

JEBBERS.

Something's wrong here.
The prairie's a flat bed
and mountains east and west bedrail his delirium.
Sometimes his fever's over 1000 feet.
He hardly knows one hip boot from another.

What can I tell you?
We're in trouble here.
The short grass prairie bobs its head
like a papoose which cannot hold itself up.

We say *HELP* and do not know where to turn.
This sick man, his head
crowded as an Appalachian bank
the first of the month.
Jeeze. He sees it all and now this road,
the years we lived on nothing.

If we give all we have:
two flints, a jean jacket, our headbands,
and say we have nothing but fields to sew up
over our graves.
If we step on the mountains
and pray to the pines,
will we CLIMB a hundred times up and down.

What if we give all this
and still have nothing?

Will it be all right
after our throats're sprayed with merthiolate,
arms jabbed with penicillin,
will we rise up then and be healed?

Hearing about the Mystery Lights on a Bus near Joplin

It's gorgeous in this southwest corner of Missouri.
The orange trees in autumn
and the *spooklights*
if you're there on the road at the right time of night.

When you first tell me about the strange lights
that appear on some dirt road
I think they're large as haywagons.
But they're small, you say.
You can almost hold them in your hand
as though lanterns carried between farmhouse and outhouse.
Or someone walking to the barn.
Or going to the chicken coop
to see if it's closed for the night.
The lights always moving, you say.
The way dead bugs on the windshield
could still be said to fly.

1.

1. (BLACK SCREEN. WIND SOUND. WOUSH. SUDDEN LIGHT. THE PRAIRIE. A LINE OF MEN ON HORSEBACK AND IN WAGONS. THEN THE NARRATOR.)

His head tossed nervous as a sunflower on a stalk. His horse jumped the gun. Maybe he couldn't stop him. Maybe he wanted to get ahead. But they shot him DEAD! One man rode ahead to catch the horse. The others carried him off. The run to unassigned lands would be square. You know the hatchet shape. The pan on the stove. A certain narrative quality. A sense of 1889. The sky with its boot-heel on the land. The land with heat-squiggles in the distance like a spectral Indian dance.

2. (SHOT OF NARRATOR BY MAKE-SHIFT TENT.)

I thought Sooners meant whoever got to the plot of land they wanted first. But no. Sooners were those who jumped the gun. Those who did and got away with it.

3. (ANOTHER NARRATOR, MYSELF, WITH A VOICE I CAN'T HOLD BACK.)

Out there in The Museum of the Western Prairie, Altus, Oklahoma. I was there when one of those blizzards hammered. Well, the afternoon it started, I was in the museum. This is only a partial list: bullet forceps, single-blade plow, a tooth extractor, a prince Albert tobacco tin. Then outside: the replica of a first house built on the treeless prairie. First you find a ravine or slope on the flat land. Dig into it. Pile rocks on top of one another for a facade. Voilà. You have a one-room house. Unload from the wagon a bed, table, chairs, kettle, cookstove. Hang dried meat and a few prairie herbs. Bake at 105 in the Oklahoma summers. Freeze-dry in winter blizzards. (QUICK TAKE ON THE BLIZZARD.)

4. (NOW THE NARRATOR LOOKS DEEP WITHIN HIMSELF FOR A VOICE. AFTER A MOMENT HE SPEAKS WITH MOVING FORETHOUGHT AND SADNESS.)

All that way
for a one-room dug-out in a ravine bank.
Then (AFTER A SCENE CHANGE WHICH I HAVE NOT
SKETCHED IN YET) a sod house.
Ridge poles driven into the hard ground to hold
the sod walls.
Buffalo-grass cut from the prairie with a sod-plow
and stacked for the walls.
Flour-sacks sewn together for a ceiling
that sifted dirt and rain.
Rats. Vermin. Snakes.
Sometimes the roof fell in, yet it holds up
the prairie sky like two hands folded
in prayer.
(HEAR THE POETIC DICTION. VERY CLEVER.)

5. (AFTER A FEW WELL-CRAFTED SCENES WE'LL BE READY FOR THE ACTION. YOU'VE SEEN THE PICTURES OF THE SOD HOUSE ON THE PRAIRIE. THE FAMILY OF 12 CHILDREN. THE OLD MAN AND WOMAN IN CHAIRS IN THE YARD. FROWNING.)

(BACK TO THE STORY WHICH I KEEP FORGETTING. ROUGH LAND, YOU KNOW. OTHER THINGS CROWD- ING IN. INDIANS HANG AROUND THE TRADING POST HOPING FOR LIQUOR. THE WOMEN WANT CALICO. THEY THINK THE EVIL SPIRITS CAN GET IN ANY ORI- FICE AND COVER THEIR EARS AND NOSE AND MOUTH. NOW THE RATTLE OF THE WAGONS AT THE STARTING SHOT. HAYWIRE EVERYWHERE.)

6. (MY OWN VOICE AGAIN. HOW WILL WE EVER GET ON WITH THIS?)

Well Oklahoma got its handle because Texas and Kansas didn't want to touch one another during the Civil War. Though I heard later that wasn't true either. But had something to do with the meridian. Anyway. I thought of it later reading in part the diary of Paul Klee. The mind made visible. The trees in abstract thought brought to concrete squiggling-lines-on-canvas.

(SEE THERE IT GOES AGAIN. I START TO SAY SOME- THING THEN BANG THERE'S A SHOT OF SOMETHING ELSE. UNEXPECTED. POETIC. DON'T YOU THINK? THOSE INDIANS WITH THE EVIL SPIRITS CRAWLING IN AND OUT THEIR NOSE. GAWL. WHAT'D YOU THINK THE PRAIRIE WAS? A PIECE OF UNINHABITED LAND? EVERYWHERE I LOOK THE SPIRITS DANCE AND WIND WHIRLS THE DUST RIGHT OFF THE GROUND.)

7. (NARRATOR AGAIN.)

You must think of them now.
Not the medicine men, but the preachers.
If you didn't buy their brimstone, you were an outcast.
A reject. Repo.
Out there on the prairie the hundreds of miles
the isolation settles in.

8. (NOW & THEN A FLASHBACK. A STAMPEDE OF HORSES'
FEET, THEIR MANES LIKE A COVEY OF BIRDS WHIPPING
THEIR NECKS.)

9. (ANOTHER POINT OF VIEW FROM THE NARRATOR,
MAYBE INTERNAL DIALOGUE. VENTRILOQUISM. A SOD
BUSTER SPEAKING TO HIS GRANDSON. THE WOODEN
KID ON HIS KNEE INTERESTED IN EVERYTHING BUT.
LOOKING MAYBE AT THE SATURDAY SKY OR DOGS
FUCKING RIGHT THERE IN THE YARD.)

We yelled at the sky to get out of the way.
We yelled at the horses.
We yelled at anything that could help us run.
The wood crates of our wagons shaking
like the Holy Ghost come down.

(HOW DO YOU LIKE THAT IMAGE?)

(THE OLD VOICE OF THE NARRATOR STILL SPEAKS.)
Fields plowed in warrior stripes.
(NO WE'RE NOT READY FOR THAT YET. SEE IT IN MY
EYES. A WHOLE LOT OF DISSATISFACTION OVER THE
WAY THINGS ARE GOING.)
The land run hardly begun.

(AND I'M FIGHTING MYSELF TO STAY OUT OF THE DUST
BOWL. A SENSE OF 1930. WE ALL KNOW IT IN THIS
AFTER-TIME WE LIVE IN. THESE EVILS GETTING UP
OUR NOSE AND CLOGGING OUR BRAINS.)

(THE NARRATOR IS TIEING OR IT IS TYING HIS HAT ON
HIS HEAD AFTER HE'S GONE TO FETCH IT NOW 12
TIMES WHILE I'M TRYING TO SHOOT.)

The first night in the awful prairie dark.
(I'M FIGHTING OFF THE INTRUSION OF OTHERS. GIVE
ME SOME HELP WON'T YOU JUST DON'T STAND THERE
WITH THE CAMERA GAWKING BUT LEND A HAND
BUSTER WHO IS PULLING ME OFF BASE OUT OF FOCUS
OUT OF WHACK?)

10. (WHAT? MY VOICE AGAIN?)
The howl of coyotes. The furrows you see run by the car like antelope
when you drive old 51 west in Oklahoma. Maybe out to Taloga
where you spend a week on another shoot. You stay in a Butler
Building which is your motel on the edge
of town in another blizzard with the flu.
You know they have dinosaur bones out
there. You bring one back and keep it in
the birch-bark bowl on your table.

(HERE WE ARE OUT OF OUR TIME-FRAME AGAIN. BUT
YOU KNOW EVERYTHING MOVES AROUND ON YOU
OUT HERE THE WIND BLOWS EVEN THE AFTERNOON
AROUND SO IT'S HERE BEFORE YOU KNOW IT WITH
NIGHT RIGHT UPON IT LIKE AN INDIAN BLANKET
WITH US UNDER IT. I'M THINKING NOW WE MAY
EVEN BE CURSED. SOMETIMES I ACTUALLY FEEL THE
REINS IN MY HANDS. THINK OF IT. WHEN I'M ASLEEP I

HEAR SOMETHING GOING ON. I FEEL THE YELL IN MY THROAT FOR THE HORSES TO RUN AHEAD TO THE LAND OUT THERE WHICH DOESN'T EVEN STAND STRAIGHT BUT WOBBLES LIKE A DRUNK INDIAN. YOU SHOOT THEM AWAY FROM THE POST BUT THEY'RE BACK. ONCE THEY TASTE LIQUOR THEY FOLLOW YOU LIKE TUMBLEWEED. YOU KNOW HOW THEY STACK UP IN TOWN AFTER A DRY SUMMER. THE WHOLE LAND GETTING READY TO BLOW AWAY. NOW THAT'S FORE-THOUGHT SPECTERING THE EVIL SPIRITS TO SEE WHAT'S COMING. NO WE'RE BETTER OFF FOR NOT KNOWING, AREN'T WE?)

(I'M PUTTING DIMES IN MY EARS AND NOSE. KEEPING THE EVIL SPIRITS OUT IF NOTHING ELSE TO PAY TO OKLAHOMA TURNPIKE TOLLS.)

Yeeow. Statehood finally. 1907.
How the dust devils dance.
I've seen them in the afternoons
that follow with cloud-marks for water-holes.
Yes. This Oklahoma where we're rewarded for trying to be there.
(THE HEAT SQUIGGLES ON THE ROAD AHEAD. THE DIARY OF PAUL KLEE STILL BESIDE ME ON THE SEAT. I LOOK THROUGH HIS DIARY AS I TRAVEL. "ONE THING IS QUITE CERTAIN: IN THE CREATIVE MOMENTS I HAVE THE GREAT PRIVILEGE OF FEELING THOROUGHLY CALM.")

11. (THE NARRATOR SPEAKS.)

Sometimes the potatoes were puff balls when we dug them from the ground. Blueberry pies would bake in an open window.

(HYPERBOLE UPON HYPERBOLE.)

12. ("A SELF THAT IS SUBJECT TO QUIVERINGS AND CONVULSIONS CHEAPENS ITS STYLE AND STEPS OUT OF THE FRAME.")

13. (THE NARRATOR WITH HIS VOICE IN ANOTHER FORM.)

I tell you I could feel the heat in my teeth. All day the sun is a heat-lamp over the house and the crop shrinks back in the ground. Turtles crawl onto the road. Trucks can't help but hit them. (THIS WILL BE LEFT UNFINISHED FOR THE MOMENT.)

14. (I CAN'T STOP THE POETIC FORCE OF THIS DRAMA ANY LONGER. BLACK SCREEN. WIND SOUND. WOUSH. SUDDEN LIGHT WHICH IS SOON COVERED WITH A THICK BLANKET OF DUST. KLEE'S PENCIL LIKE A TOR-NADO ON THE PRAIRIE. SEVERAL OF KLEE'S PENCILS LIKE GREAT CLOUDS OF DUST. THE NARRATOR HOLDS TO A RURAL ELECTRICITY POST AS HE SPEAKS.)

The 30's dust bowl.
WPA bridges.
Not a fuzzle of water in the cricks.
Workclothes flapping on the line.
You can see dust fry.

15. (QUITE A JUMP IN TIME THERE. I MAY HAVE TO HANDLE IT DIFFERENTLY.)

All I know
my heart's in this now
jiggling like buckshot
in a Prince Albert tobacco tin.

Bluzzard

"IT GRADUALLY BECAME A DIFFERENT COUNTRY."

—*John Koethe, "Morning in America"*

The days shiber like toast when it shook
the room.
We'd knowd them like the names of sheeb.
They twist up there in the sky,
pusht nord under the ceiling light,
the closet shelb.
Does anyone find the heaps of stars
shut like a cellar?
The folds of light in waves on the shore?
We'd know what to do
if we weren't in this icebox
of a country getting clost to winter.

God's blessing's on this continent. YEZ. Which rhymes with rez. Well. Uncle Zebo driving the Queen Elizabeth Way from Detroit to Ontario. Gets off somewhere in Niagara with his camera. That's what he does. Soon as he gets his money he doesn't go for groceries but gasoline. Then he's off sometimes with someone with him. Or a hitchhiker. He's the only one I know still picks them up. The latest postcard's from El Paso. He's on Rim Road looking down on Juarez. Said the power of the blessing's with him there. *Wop.* Like the lime oil cloth on the rez table. He writes his treatment. Takes the shots. This new age has left us all so open-mouthed. We count on him over the white-wall moon. Saying *Love from Crab Daddy in the jet stream.*

Flight 532 - Houston to Mpls

"AH WONDER WHAR PAPPY GOT LOST."

—*Mammy Yokum*

Y ou know there's rain that falls so high it dries before it gets to earth. You see it spill from clouds on a high flight. And one spook of a cloud with its ladle stirring a backyard kettle. But you leave it spinning in the afterdraft of the plane. Thinking you're going so fast. The line of a highway. The squiggle of a river far below. Splots of ponds all up and down the horizon like neon cafes. The clouds are a pop-up landscape white and flaky. Saying *Spaz City*. HEY. Feel the brain coral in your head. Where pools of the sky open up. The roads getting farther and farther away from America. The clouds of their washing toward the horizon. You may jump up and down in your boots. But that's what you're facing. The moving of America under you. All over the spangled earth the ponds SPARKLE as the sun spreads its marmalade across them saying HEY we're down here. YES we're here. And a river like a piece of bread crust hangs from the sky. It's hazy when you look from the plane. 37,000 FEET on a summer evening and you kick the sides of the plane with your spurs to go faster. 2 1/2 hours where the clouds are white candle-holders marked *Made in Mexico* you almost bought in Texas. And you're in a grove of mangos. The ground somewhere down there in the white mass that used to be America. The way possibly the continent was first formed under the stirring hands. And you see the Fathers of the Constitution in the thunderheads on the horizon. And the white steamy vapor from Mammy Yokum's pot. Another pond's off there in the distance. You think maybe the whole glorious sticky earth's still down there. You say OKAY BUCKO. One more dance. Forgetting the curios in souvenir stores. The pick-up stix game you had as a child and nobody plays anymore. Even you were bored because it was something you couldn't do. Maybe nobody could. Pick up stix from the pile without moving.

Two Forms, *Henry Moore, Philadelphia Museum of Art*

I think Ben Franklin lived in Philadelphia, and all they taught us about history between the children's voices and the small birds on those chilly days on the playground. I would like to say there was another history. Before our easement into civilization. I see it in the two stone forms. Child-sized, they are short pillars or mono-liths. One has a single eye and both are marked with a few Kandinsky hieroglyphics as if xrayed after swallowing a coil and some needle-thin lines. And the absent arms? Just less weight car-ried under the blanket. The two forms are the stone ghosts of my Cherokee ancestors, not riding high on horses in parks, nor stand-ing like Wm. Penn on the dome of a building looking up his own tree-lined avenue. But the two forms inside the museum are small and shrunken as limbs not used. They are the invisible ones in his-tory class polished without features. Weren't people smaller then anyway, as though they could wear the wool dress I washed once? I think of the looper caterpillar we used to watch on the playground. Its frantic saw-like march. We poked it with a stick, knocked it over when it arched, set it upright again, finally squished it flat as history. Now I turn back to Moore's sculpture and the one eye is a navel and the two forms are legs of the ancestors walking 10 miles a day for 900 hundred miles from Georgia to Indian Territory in winter. There, far from Independence Hall, the stamina and consti-tution that was theirs.

Muling America cherrier all the time
your kudzu covers the world
nightshift America turning all 4's
assembly line prodigy
child star
moving field of fuel pumps \ pistons \ cylinders
crank shafts
your highways lined with maintenance shops
junk yards when the cost is more than the keep
rum rum
go White Castle Hamburger
go American Royalty
dream 3 branches
Ford \ Chevy \ American Motors
honk the pokeys
generous America \ a car for each
rush hour's a Bill of Rights
and democracy is wheels away.

Giving the Air Away

Science tells you an apple falls because of gravity \
History \ how many times (& where) the mov't of mass
through space \ But Art (ah!) \ revelation rather than
analysis \ The downfall of an apple \ death of civili(zation) \
The leap of us all (and how the passage downward
is fast in our fast time) \ Oh precious America \
fol(lowing) an apple \ your balloon not so full \ It's
easier (isn't it?) \ Now you can let go (except for those
straggling in excellence) \ You were front runner \ Chief
\ Now you take a second seat in the world \ Your
di(versity)! \ Your wild charity.

Cinnamon Bear, Field Museum, Chicago

It's how we take the animals \ put some in baseball caps \ stick others in museums \ and there he is right inside the door \ open under the atrium \ his claws held up \ his head tilted toward the branching glass of the ceiling. He stands on his squat hind legs \ nearly extinct from our continent \ as if still reaching for a hive. In the next room the buffalo fade patiently \ thousands of them shot from passing trains \ riddled with holes like the boards from a garage roof in Benld, Illinois, where a meteorite fell in 1938 ripping into the seat of a Pontiac coup \ even the dented muffler is there on a wing of the second floor between fossils & skeletons \ and downstairs a bear \ his massive body raised as if to catch the next. Out across the shore of Lake Michigan a boat roars through the water \ really fast jumping waves \ sometimes it comes all the way out of the water \ I can see light under it \ the motor & propeller like testicles I saw on a dog walking in the park \ the pointed boat \ the shaft of it passing through the mind \ why shouldn't it? And the pigeon in the street with heat stroke or his feet run over \ he couldn't walk but flayed by the curb. The anger \ the expelling this life \ this pain. What does the bear do all night? What does he do in winter when he's deprived of hibernation? Has his soul departed to the hunting grounds? Is that it now \ that shadow he's reaching for through the glass?

After-Image

He watched her haunches,
rapped the last pine tree he saw
in the mountains.
But now they were in the great basin.
The sun hardly up sank as a wet, red mass
ahead of them. All day the horses
pulled the heavy load heaving under the yokes
and she was one of them. He had seen her born.
Had cried at the first gangly steps.
Watching the stifle, gaskin, hock.
Now she stood in line with the horses.
Not flaunting herself
but pulling, always just head of the wagon.
He trembled a little
as short grasses waved.
Oh, the quick round eye.
The scissor-like legs that opened the air.

Black Hawk

We know the mountains are heavy
with afternoon rain
and have heaved a thousand years
or at least an afternoon of door to door
heavy deliveries
from the brown UPS truck
hurrying
between the shiny bracelets
on the long arms of the town.
The mountains, the valleys between them.
Oh great America
I hold you up.
The street shops,
their fine bells and beveled glass.
A spangled carpet with a small rodent carrying
magic mirrors full of a bright flash of hope.

Point Reyes Peninsula, California

This is as far as they could go.
Through plains. Badlands. Mountain pines.
Finally the land bends backward from
the coast, saying, *WOAH!* to horses and wagons.
They still crowd the steep path
down to the water, as though stairs
to the potato cellar. They don't quite know
what to do, backed up when waves SLAM the door.
They've come so far, they can let up
a little now. Take the staves of wagons,
make tents against the wind. The fog
stacked up like hay in a loft. Remember
how in struggle they grew strong.
Their smooth kneecaps worn as stones.

American Leaf

There were leaves everywhere that autumn.
They came from far away and stayed with friends.
Their orange flames pow-wowed in circles.

It's leaving your head
against the Missouri limestone river-bluffs
to have been there once.

The river cold and hungry for our company.
I loved those trees that time of year.
The autumn like the spell that fell over us

walking near the edge of the river.
My friend and I visiting his brother-in-law
who took us south from Columbia to Easely

and we followed a path by the shore.
I hadn't been there in thirty years
but carried those memories of trees by the river.

The leaves falling around us.
Volumes of red. Orange. Burgandy. Yellow. Russet.
Some still green, grass-dancing like wind

on the rump of a map.
They were campfire-leaves in love with their own flames.
Or leaves on a yearly migration to winter camp

as if pebbles along the river kicked by currents.
There was a heron at the river when we walked.
My friend's brother-in-law saw it first.

I forgot how wide and fast the water.
That quiet moving river almost level with our path
reflecting rows of trees on the other side.

You know the stories of river spirits
who tangle fishing lines and twirl eddies under row-
boats, not to cause us trouble, no,

but just to be near us
they lick the undersides of our boats,
the toes of our fishing boots.

I could have stayed there until night offered its corn-
pollen to the trees.
I could say to the trees

I would blow the sun back farther north in winter
if it would keep you red.
I would rake the leaves into constellations of towns

on a map if they would stay.
The clouds spread their eagle-wings above us.
I could tell my friend of the power

of their feather-bustle pattern.
The wide river-bottom messed with leaves.
Military insignias from the arms of bluffs.

I could hear the trees playing their flutes that autumn.
Trees with watermelon leaves. Cantaloupe.
I could eat you, trees. I could spread you

with my tongue. I could taste your ketchup leaves.
Some of you, yes, brilliant and fancy-dancing
in regalia your grandmothers worked on,

your mothers stayed up late finishing.
Tribes of boxelder, postoak, maple, elm, hawthorne,
willow, spruce, sweetgum, pine.

Something like all the cars on the road
with different license plates.
The grand entry of autumn in beads and jingle-dresses

I could tell my friend.
The canned pineapple of the pow-wow announcer's voice
over the microphone

honoring veterans who are not forgotten.
No, the drum of memory reminds us
as we walk the Missouri autumn.

Our heads in the gray hairs of cottonwoods.
The russet redgrape leaves as many as the stars.

A Walk on a Country Road 16 Miles
Northeast of Iowa City

An iron wagon wheel leans against a tree in a tall clump of weeds. I see it when I walk every evening and want it the way you want something that is a part of history, that has a life you haven't touched, yet you recognize it. Here on the country road between the air and the unclear ground at dusk, lightning bugs fly above the fields, lights blinking. It's not only the wagon wheel I want, but the circular shape, the overall heaviness. It's divided by spokes, cut like a pie as if Solomon had not had wisdom with the two mothers who claimed the same baby. *There are boundaries* as the dog tells me when I walk. His bark says *there are rules, there are places I can't go.* But his tail wags as though it's only his duty. The birds also fuss, flying like gliders, wary of their nests in ditches packed with weeds. Now the road cuts into a slight hill. I hear the hum of the highway in the distance. I see the steeple of the country church where on Sunday evenings we study Romans to guard against the life of the flesh. But when a friend visits I tell him about the wheel, how it hauled some wagon overland. The bones of the horses that pulled it somewhere under cornrows. Later we walk down the road and I show him the wheel. He gets his pickup about 10:00 when the farmers along the road are watching the news. We roll the wheel through the tall grasses. He lifts it into the back of the truck, closes the tailgate and we drive off with the wheel once more crossing land.

Quartet No. 5, Ernest Bloch

We've loosened the fence a little.
The forefathers would hardly know.
The evening buzzes a wasp nest.
The moon bumps against the dark.
After the whittling it's what's left.
Storms erupt from the west,
throw light from the backdoor
like water from a basin.
Outside a shed stands on one leg.
Somewhere in the dark
one-legged on a perch
the heart of America blinking
like a hen-eye in the homeland.

A Burger To Go

Physicists can't go back to the first time in our moments. We're an evening train rushing on its tracks toward dark. But that's later now we're the outward flow still traveling from the bang of one particle until cut-off. Even John on Patmos wired doom. Maybe the train turns in its roundhouse as skin rubbed off finally heals. All of life's force. Why is there this car in America instead of nothing? Clouds swirling wind and rain onto the road. You simply feel the Spirit like the turn of a mower over the yard. You believe the whatsoever. The night rain sweeps across the narrow highway and the trucks coming toward you drive water into your windshield. You know those moments you can't see where you're going. And you throw your spear into your yard 300 miles ahead and follow it as though the washouts were not there. As though your car were on track. But how do you say you survive? By faith in the force of what you don't know? That invisible hand always there holding your car. Everywhere is the center of the universe. This kernel exploded and moving outward still. Space filling with itself. Farther. Farther. A light beside the road. The dying universe where the stars. Possibly even the atoms do not survive.

Debt

You make wings in the shed
all night
you stand like a birdman
at the prow of our dreams
I hear the flaps of your wings
pulling the boat forward in the crops
the moon of your face
above the field of covers
Unamack
chief
tell me what you see
beyond the plumage of your head
aren't the sockets of our face worn
from the beating of your wings
what carnivorous god are you
hovering over us at night
leaving at dawn
with a blood bubble on your lip?

How in Spite of Us It Works

"A NEED TO FILM NOSTALGIA CREPT INTO THE STUDIO."
—*Barbara Guest, "Motion Pictures: 6"*

Someday you'll talk and I will know the weeds you sat in \ what you thought in the sway of iris at the basement window \ their migration under your eyes without moving \ The precision of your jump \ just how you calculated it \ the four white feet \ I will tell you how I traveled and saw the field of Holsteins and missed you \ black & white spotted cat \ You could sit all day \ sleep at night against my back \ I will ask how you had strength to go on no matter what \ The stamina you received like fleas \ How you watched the milkweed open their cathedrals on the fence and fly like angels \ How the thing is to get broken \ to feel a hundred fragments rush from your chest knowing they scatter to other yards to break apart in the soil \ I think of you on the road somewhere if you got lost \ crippled \ terrified \ maggots in your eyes \ How the sparkling world is a hell to some on the outside \ I will ask how you sat with dignity after the dog chased you \ and the male cat bit you again & again because he could run faster \ You'll tell me how you cleaned your gentle whiskers after you ripped apart a bird \ Your fur that shone like a snowy field in the neighbor's light when we sat on the porch in the dark \ How I would think of Christ forgotten on the cross \ all things you brought \ the patience \ forbearance \ concentration \ contentment \ How all the corners of America pointed to your moving ears.

The Hands

I think they belong to something else
moving like field-grass along the road in autumn.
I'm not sure what they should do.
Maybe nothing.
At least the hands do not remember like the heart.
Look at the ropes of the fingers.
Section-hands in a field, baling hay, let's say.
Dried mud-swirls like fingerprints at the gate.

It's here along the road continuous as the sky,
the hands move like wind flapping good-bye.
If they could only be together forever
in their large family.

Whenever I'm alone I look at them.
Out here, the country turns pale as dust on the dashboard
of the car.
The grass-cutter in the median raises a finger of dust
behind him
as if to say here the hands take root,
here the knuckles fold beneath the hills.

The terrain of the heart is threshed
by black fingers of a blown tire in the road.
Black rivulets of taped music thrown out like streamers.
Now the fingers hold one another.

Patient cows by the barn.
This is where the hands hold the blades of grass
between the chewing of the fingers,
not knowing, but trusting the only law they know.

I remember how your hands worked patiently that time
a pigeon fell into the chimney
and cried from the ledge just above reach.
You tried for days to leg him,
then weakened and no longer fighting,
you put your hand silently into the dark,
felt his body, and brought him into the room.
How you talked to him with finger language.
How you carried him to the door.
Just a pigeon in the palms of your hands
like a morning glory.
His wings clapping into the distance.

I remember once
a man interpreting at a poetry reading.
His signs came just after the words for them.
Not unlike,
no just opposite, a man chopping wood in the distance
whose chopping-sounds come just after the movements.

Over there the turning of the autumn trees:
red maples \ sumac \ yellow oak.
The same hands still waving,
not asking for the sky they cannot hold.

Bare fingers with circles at the joints
like stones dropped into a pond.

No these hands can't be mine.
They follow the law of obedience below the heart,
steady as a tractor moving in a field.

I remember the leaves I picked up on the sidewalk
and pressed under a book.
But afterwards their edges still curled
like hands reaching out of the table,
asking for whatever it is hands want.

No. The hands do not want.
They don't feel sorrow or loss.
They're humble servants at the wheel of the car.
They could be children holding an orange pumpkin
at a roadside stand.
Once I bought some ears of red-corn
with husks standing up like fingers.
"Without my glasses," you said, *"they look like hands."*
I want you still to hold my hand,
the moving fingers.
The Morse Code of the center-line they tap.

Yes. The hands do what they're told.
They wave.
They stay in the unison of their groups.
They know the church.
The steeple.
The child's game that finds the people.

Thur's the way out.
Ars! Relief.
Whar faith, bedrock of our country
pops like french-fry grease.
Keeping knocking on.
Thur drive-through winder opuns.
Indian bead found in a creek.
Pop bottle in the ditch.
Har's cowboys on coke glasses,
A Saturday arfternoon of matinees.
One way er n'uther
cars nert tunnels
on the road (sic) hock.
What coo be do?
Yar order:
a quarter-pounder wid cheeze
over these steeples
of *Amarca*.

A Script Called Birth

Words stay trapped behind the bars of the ribs, camped out like pigeons against the foundation of the house in below zero weather.

I watch the pigeons as the temperature goes down. Finally at night, I lean a box against the house over the two of them that stay.

Next morning, they move out and hover against the foundation next door. Other pigeons spend the day mourning the loss of grass under snow, the insects, or whatever is pigeon food.

But it's the two of them, the small one I see now can't fly, I cover each night. And finally at 12 below they stay.

They're the ones in the philosophy of the earth's exclusion: survival of the fittest. I give it some resistance so they'll stay like the memory of my grandmother, the words she never spoke.

The same silence when the Marines invade Panama. The renegade general holding on after he's voted out. What can I say? Inheritor of silence. *Hang onto your life, son. There's pigeons here doing as well.*

In the morning, I hear the small one screech as the other leaves and returns, his beak thrust into her mouth for food. He flaps his wings to see if they will lift him. Then the mother could return to the eave, and not worry about a pigeon under a box where the cat could get him, except in this weather the cat stays in the house

under the covers in a warm bed. And the pigeons have only them-
selves in the cold. The feathers on their back.

Finally if it gets any colder the vigil will be over for her. But it
doesn't work that way. He fights to stay on top like the general
thumbing his nose to the big country north of him.

It's why on Christmas day at dinner, I cry and can't stop. The
turkey and potatoes in my mouth, the tears running down my face,
and how the next morning my uncle shows me a poem in a book I
gave him for Christmas. How a man cried in the attic of his house
because of the beauty, the awfulness of this life. The trees holding
up, the snow falling, the both of them to show me he understands.

No, it can't be said. The private language wrapped in tears. The
ordinary beauty of the family, the son who's a Marine. Don't think
about it, the glory of America, the snow sparkling. His late-year
birth remembered by a man-hole cover much like a black scab over
the navel when we stand by the curb after the water-main breaks
and floods the street after a cold spell, and gives the world its water
like the pigeon feeding her young from her own throat.

Anthem

America gracious land
in the center a miniature figure
with nails in its hands.
You can open the workings of law
of gov't
the past that holds slow starts
now with a quick bang
you leap to the front of the show.
Woe to the competition
it would be years
the waxed fruit
the silly varnishes
all thin as curtains
in the back room the fallen leaves
the federalist papers
on the lawn
the struggle that somehow
comes out right.

Gerald

Tubes of clouds cross the evening sky. I would put my finger on them, hold them from leaving, but everything here moves.

You jerk the gears of the borrowed truck. All that heavy furniture across the city, into a new door and other rooms.

For some reason I think of my son who once dreamed of another child, Gerald, who was never born.

If only memory were a pink light in which we turned lovely with these clouds from the broad windshield of the truck.

The clouds remind me of the tubes in old department stores when I bought a handkerchief with my mother and our money was put in a small casing that went to the money changer somewhere above and soon returned with a receipt for the handkerchief.

No time is only now, but a cycle come back. I remember how peace never came nor really anything we wanted, yet the family endured on the edge of the land where all things diminish and yet my parents made it barely speaking sometimes and how that same strain broke my marriage. Now with someone else, the same move, the same tasks.

These pink clouds rush toward a changing light. All that daylight slowly fading from us now, but comes and goes like mystery lights that appear on the country road.

We lie down in our beds. Always the downward pull of earth, the longing of it for us until finally it pulls us back into itself.

Daddums. You plow through the skin of river while money rises and returns when we had all day to take the bus to town.

An open air market. Festival tents like wings of pigeons over awnings on old department stores. I remember white napkins blowing from booths like gloved hands. The water across the same spillways. Already fields and orchards of the next year push through.

So many days pass we hardly keep count of them any more than turns of the revolving door until we find ourselves at the start of another century. And how always moving this country goes its way with alternate layers of light and dark, or tenderness and anger, still nearly always laughing, nearly always close to dreams of a child just under the ribs.

When the gate to the Philippine Marine base closed
I breathed easier. All ships
out on the little sea. Men down in them

you can't see. But the hot general
trooping it up in the desert. Looking under
invisible leaves. Now he calls

ships from rushing dozed. Out on the flat
oceanic glowlamp which the night-
gulf is. Tell me where you are or even one part

of your face that froze to silkworms
on the screen. Not Marines under the leaves
of island pandanus. But the seeming

tasklessness of those waiting for the night-
birds cooing. The wings
of helicopters soon to float over the desert.

The long blades like praying mantisses sewed
to the deck. The one duty still divided
between the hit and the blows.

America

What a place
all the swell guns the tomahawks
stepping your big foot in
where Geronimo wouldn't.

Great America
all right
so you did it
you made party favors and confetti of the land
yo sorties
yo bunkers
what are those helicopters called
the fast ones
you know that come in off the boats
out there in the Gulf?

Put it down then
get right in with all your feet
light of nations
blow-torch of the world.

Military Briefing

It was the lonest day
to stand by itself out there.
Sameness was everywhere.
The stringlights always on the sky.
The dark alone received them.
It was hard you know.
The cups of teepees like snowcones.
The coils of clouds hanging on a nail.
It was a tunest day.
Even the airfields the planes hissed over.
Reconnoitering in sand
thousands of miles away.

I think she was spoken into existence. Because my children were
gone, and the man I was married to. Perhaps in a dream I said to
the empty room, *animal you come in here you stay,* and we agreed.
The words that made her sometimes drop from her fur. She licks
herself as if she felt a slight prick where they left, or as if she had to
smooth back her fur they ruffled. A four-legged marked with black
soot from ancient ceremony. Or marked as if the darkness held on
too long when she stepped into light, or turned back a moment to
see where she'd come from. A fight between day and night, or
good and evil. *It's still that way in the world* when I tell her, *animal
we will pray,* and I hear her voice, *zum roto. Yo roto,* she keeps say-
ing, and I move her with my foot to let her know it's my domain
we're praying for. It's my prayers we're saying. The word is our
maker, but now it separates. I feel her rough tongue over the edges
that hurt. But there's more now than just that. We speak to the
whipped-up battery of soldiers on some hot border. In her purr I
hear the tanks roar distantly over the sand. I hear old war chiefs
buzz. The story never changes. Their sweaty ghosts stick. I say to
her *we are in that darkness again. We can put our hand upon it, feel its
teeth.* But I tell her *there's a power that expells us. There's a power that
speaks us back to light.*

This Morning

There are cut flowers in a carafe on the table.
The stalks are engorged by the water
and the curve of glass.
There is one leaf floating in the vase,
an army green.
As I turn the vase I see there are other leaves.
They become waving flags.
Above the water
the stalks are a forest of flag poles in disarray.
Voluming upward.
Over there, these flowers could be for graves
or those lost in their ships at sea.
Just above the water-line
a leaf is pressed to the neck of the carafe
like the last note of a piano
or some voice underwater.
But the flowers are full and pure and white
reverberating with nothing
except maybe the image of hens
on the trellis of their perch.
Tell me what they mean.
The fragrant heads blooming now like clouds.
The stalks underwater as if thin green cartridges
shoved into the magazine of the carafe.

But this morning
there's refracted light from the window
in distorted panels of heaven.
And there's the sound of a flute.
All noise the night my daughter in 6th-grade band
played *The Battle Hymn of the Republic,*
the trumpets and flutes pointed like guns
on a battleship
or the long trombones of the tanks.
Now the green fingers lift,
arms really,
as if receiving the returning,
as if saying, *we have survived.*

The Day Before Christmas

I look at the car we're passing
and get a flash in the eye,
an unbelievable snapshot
of the family reunion in my face.
And there on the fields
the white snow staying behind after a storm.
The child I used to be responsible for
is driving me back to an aunt's house
for Christmas,
the only place left we have to go.
His new truck with shocks wound tightly,
a camouflage of 4-wheel drive.
In the backwindow, *'Marines'*
jitters over each crack on Interstate 35.
Some western mama on the tape deck
love-broken by the truth of ideas.
Now the clouds break-up
over South Skunk and Middle River.
The ice pieces at the side of the road
are something like lint balls
or minute tumbleweed
or thorns handed from another day
hurting the fingers.
Nine hours on the road.
Optical illusions, these circles of light,
haloes or eyelets of small fists

or buttonholes from a sun high in the heavens.
I tell him to slow down
in the wash of melted ice over the highway,
that preview of afterlife,
its angling torn from the perforation of time.
Look at the grassbrown tiretracks
in the snow on a field.
A farmer's conclave
asking if this is all we're here for.
These flights toward the sun
reflecting windshield-glass and metal.
These diagonal lapses into the sea
with our wax-shines,
our flesh-and-bone wings.

The Relief of America

In stepping back from the world and looking at it from a distance, in North America they took a light from our fire and carried it over and lighted their fire. And there was a great light of peace because that's what they said they followed. If you saw the earth from a distance back then, you would see this brilliance, and then it began to die. They refused to use the spirit as part of their nation. They said they had to separate church and state, and surely they did. But the church they brought was not spirit in the same way. It was built on doctrine and power over the people. Not the power of the people in their own hands. No, you have to separate their church and state. But it was America's high point. 1776. The light shooting up from the Continental Congress and the Six Nation Iroquois Confederacy when they talked. With B. Franklin taking notes. Until the stuff they brought from over the sea reasserted itself, and the light died more. To say it again, we swing between our poles, and it takes the spirit to strike balance between. You name the tenents of justice / peace / community / accountability / over the long haul of topography. The light can come back, what a relief, if you could have seen America from that distance in time.

—Paraphrased from Oren Lyons, Faith Keeper of the Onondaga Nation